AF259228

The 100 Funniest Parenting Truths of All Time

The 100 Funniest Parenting Truths of All Time

VICTOR JUNIOR

When choosing your first diaper bag, be sure to purchase one with lots of extra pockets to hold all your hopes and dreams for the next 18-25 years.

Once you sign-on
to be a mom,
the only shift on offer is
"On-call 24/7"

Life with a newborn
is a lot like college life.

Everything's a mess,
nobody's slept in days,
and there's a chance
someone could puke
on you at any moment.

Parenting a newborn is a lot
like being a pilot on Day 1.

No experience,
no training,
but lives are at stake.

The first month of parenting a newborn will prove that you can do just about anything - with one hand.

70% of parenting a newborn
is thinking about when you
can next lie down.

You officially become a
"mom/dad" when
your child is born.

You officially become a
"parent" when leaving the
house by yourself is
considered a vacation.

Moms don't want
to sleep like a baby.

They want to sleep
like their husband.

Inside your purse will be pictures of your children - where your money and freedom used to be.

Parenting Tip:

Athleisure Wear

Parenting a newborn
is a lot like Burning Man
and Coachella.

Random puking,
no showers,
sensory overload,
and wearing the same
underwear for 3-7 days.

Fun Fact:

"Naptime" is less for them
and more for you.

Thought of the Day:

There is only one really
beautiful child in the world -
and every mom has it.

Hell hath no fury like
a toddler whose sandwich
was cut into triangles
when they asked for squares.

When your toddler wants to
"show you something"
be prepared for them
to place it directly
inside your eye socket.

No matter how tired
or busy you are,
when a toddler hands you
a ringing toy phone,
you take the call.

83% of a mom's daily caloric intake comes from licking knives and eating leftovers.

Having one child
makes you a parent.

Having 2 or more
makes you a referee.

"Uhh... because it's magic!" is a perfectly valid response when your toddler asks you something you don't know the answer to.

If you're not ~~bribing~~ incentivising during potty training, you're not doing it right.

Thought of the Day:

One day you will be
thankful that your child
is strong-willed.

But today is not that day.

Cherish the day you upgrade the "family car" because it will be the last day the floor isn't covered in Cheerios and Goldfish.

Parenting Tip:

When your toddler asks
for "2 more minutes",
always agree.

They have
no concept of time.

#MomHack

Do not underestimate
the power of a brightly
colored Paw Patrol Band-Aid
to heal even the most
non-existent of ouchies.

Cherish the short vacations
away from your kids.

Like when you put them in
their child seat, close the
door, and walk around
to the driver's seat.

Fun Fact:

Kids can smell when you start relaxing.

"So I turned my back for, like, two seconds…" is how every "parenting a toddler" story begins.

Savour the years your children can't read before they realise you've only been reading 15% of their bedtime stories.

Don't discuss your
"dog problems"
with parents.

Your dog doesn't shout
"Hey, mom!"
11,000 times a day.

Once you're a parent
you'll finally understand
why they're called
"throw pillows"

Be prepared to explain
WHY red is your favourite color
and HOW T-Rex's used the
toilet before toilet paper
was invented.

Kids will forget how
to tie their shoelaces,
but will remember the
candy bar you promised
them 7 weeks ago if they
were quiet in the car
that you never paid up.

The definition of
"Parenting a toddler":

Surviving each day until the
kid's bedtime, then watching
the first 2.5 minutes of a Netflix
show before passing out.

9 times out of 10,
sentences that begin with
"Well, my daddy always says…"
do NOT end well.

"That's so interesting!"
is a perfectly valid response
to the 8-minute story your
toddler just told
that you weren't
listening to.

Cleaning Tip:

Folding laundry
with a toddler nearby
is like raking leaves
in a hurricane.

Fun Fact:

Come bedtime, every toddler
transforms into a dehydrated,
singing philosopher
who only thrives on hugs.

To help get through the day, think of your toddler as the personification of a 3'2" middle finger.

Kids will not hear you shout
their name the first 2-3 times,
but will hear you open a
candy bar wrapper,
under your pillow,
from the other side
of the house.

Nothing will test your
immune system like
a toddler sneezing
directly into your cornea.

Fun Fact:

Toddlers inherit karate skills
at age 3 and instinctively
Van Damme the bathroom
door the exact moment
you start peeing.

When you tell your child
"Yes, in a minute"
what you're really saying is
"Please forget what
you asked me".

As a parent, you will have
the power to ruin your
toddler's day by simply
asking them to put
on their other sock.

We'd all like to be perfect "Instagram & Pinterest Moms", but sometimes "Take-out Dinner & Amazon Prime Moms" are just as good.

Becoming a parent involves
speaking in the Royal "We".
eg. "No, we don't eat
the dog's food" or
"No, we don't need to wash
daddy's keys in the toilet."

Nothing screams we're going to be 3 hours late like a toddler demanding "I can do it by myself."

Parenting Tip:

Netflix "Autoplay" Mode

Fun Fact:

Adults have between
5-6 different sleep positions.

Toddlers who co-sleep
have approximately 147.

Parenting Tip:

Wrap empty boxes in wrapping paper and place them under the Christmas tree.
When a child misbehaves, throw a present into the fireplace and shout "That's one down…!"

A toddler will achieve
more in two unsupervised
minutes than you will
in a whole day.

Thought of the Day:

Einstein once said,
"The definition of parenting is
doing the same thing over
and over, but expecting
different results."

(Wait… or was that insanity?)

"Don't eat things you
find under the couch!"
is just one of the fun things
you never thought
you'd have to shout,
but will.

The definition
of "torture":

Watching your toddler try
to zip their jacket
on their own.

Living with a toddler is
a lot like a singles bar:

Everything is sticky,
the same music is played on
loop and someone could
puke on you at any moment.

60% of parenting is shouting "But you just had a snack!" over and over until you finally give in and get them another snack.

Fun Fact:

The names of your child's
kindergarten classmates
will sound a lot like
Instagram filters

You are officially a parent when you develop the instinct to catch your child's throw-up in your bare hands.

Fun Fact:

The average adult speaks about 10,000 words/day.

The average toddler achieves this by 8:17 am.

Parenting is that
grey area between
"Put that down" and
"Fine. What's the worst
that could happen."

"Mom's Iced Coffee" Recipe

1. Make a hot coffee
2. Have children
3. Forget that you made said coffee
4. Drink it cold 4hrs later

Serves: 1

Fun Fact:

A toddler is equally
impressed by a $200 toy
as they are by an oversized
tree branch they
found at the park.

When you ask your kids to "get dressed" what they actually hear is "Please loiter semi-naked in front of the TV while holding one sock."

#MomHack

The quickest way to get your child's attention is to sit down and look comfortable

Add "okay sweetheart?"
to the end of any statement
to make it sound more loving.
eg. "Please stop that or
mommy will leave you
here in the field,
okay sweetheart?"

The sole purpose of giving your child a middle name is so they know when they're really in trouble.

Parenting Tip:

Wine in a coffee cup.

Thought of the Day:

If evolution really existed,
why do moms still
only have two hands?

When you start to lose your
patience with your kids,
take a slow deep breath
and remind yourself:
They'll choose your
nursing home one day.

Watching grandparents interact with their grandchildren is like watching the childhood you never had play out right in front of you.

Parenting Tip:

The stronger your child's will,
the stronger your
drink should be.

Cooking Tip:

If they're old enough to critique your cooking, they're old enough to cook for themselves.

Fun Fact:

78% of parenting is making empty threats.

Just when you think you have
this parenting thing under
control, your kid will come
home from school
with a recorder.

Cooking Tip:

You will reach a point where your children's dinner menu will consist of two choices:

Take it or leave it

There is nothing wrong with burning one side of their toast, serving it the other side up and crossing your fingers.

Kids have
two volume levels:

Mute, and
"So Loud I Can't
Hear Myself Think"

Moms have
two volume levels:

Normal, and
"So Loud Even The
Neighbours Are Brushing
Their Teeth and Putting
On Their Pajamas"

When the children have
frayed your last nerve,
remember that chocolate
and ice-cream always work.

And the kids like them too.

You are officially a parent when
you've said "I love you too"
with a soft undertone of
disgust and anger.

The definition
of "fast":

A parent eating something
they don't want to share.

Thought of the Day:

Your love for your children will be infinite.

Your patience will not.

If your child wants to run around with you and play "race cars", explain that you blew your alternator and that the replacement part needs to be shipped from Italy with a 7-10 day lead time.

Then just lay there and do nothing.

"… with soap!"
is a fun addendum you'll
need to shout whenever
your kids wash their hands.

In your 20's, you questioned
whether 3:49 am was
too early to go home.

As a parent, you'll question
whether 6:38 pm is
too early to go to bed.

Threatening to bag up all their toys and donate them will not be your proudest moment – but will be a necessary evil.

#MomHack

3 minutes = the appropriate amount of time to help your child look for their chocolate that you ate last night.

Fun Fact:

Come snack times and
mealtimes, dads don a
cloak of invisibility so only
moms can deal with
any and all requests.

60% of parenting is waiting
for your kids to go to bed
so you can watch shows
with nudity and eat junk.

When you say "No"
what your children hear is
"Ask me again. I didn't
quite understand you."

If you ever feel like you've failed as a parent, remind yourself that the mom in E.T. had an alien living in her son's closet for 2 week before she noticed anything.

Moms take
2 types of showers:

The 1-minute
"Splash the Main Bits"

and

The 17-minute
"Questioning My Life Choices
While Standing Motionless"

If you're too tired
to clean the house,
watch an episode of
"Hoarders" and feel good
about yourself.

You are officially a parent when you develop the instinct to know you're already late for something that doesn't start for 6 hours.

Never speak about yourself
as a "failure of a parent"

...in front of your children.

If you're considering having more than one child, just know that siblings *always get along.

*As long as they're not playing together, looking at each other, near each other, in the same house, or breathing the same air.

Fun Fact:

When your child confides that they had a bad dream, declaring "Reality is scarier" does not defuse the situation.

When your children become
teenagers, get a dog.

It's important to have
someone in the house
that's happy to see you.

55% of parenting is reminding your kids how much more time they have left of something.

If you can't find your teenagers, change the WiFi password and they'll find you.

Cleaning the house with your children still in it is like brushing your teeth while eating chocolate cake.

The hardest
part of parenting is
maintaining a fake "mad face"
when what your child does
is wrong, but hilarious!

Final Thought of the Day:

For maximum effectiveness,
Advil bottles recommend
taking 1-2 tablets every
4 hours and to Keep Away
From Children

FROM THE AUTHOR

Thanks for reading *The 100 Funniest Parenting Truths of All Time*!

I *really* hope you enjoyed it!

As a small business owner (and self-employed writer) my Amazon reviews and ratings are paramount for my success and growth.

So if you can spare a minute to leave a positive Amazon review it would go a long way towards helping others decide about my book.

Thank you so much (in advance)! And all jokes aside, always remember:

- The days are long, but the years are short.

- There's no such thing as a perfect parent. Just do your best.

- And always kiss your children goodnight.
  (Even if they're already asleep.)

See you in my next book!

CHECK OUT OUR OTHER TITLES:

THE 100 GREATEST DAD JOKES OF ALL TIME

THE 100 FUNNIEST KIDS JOKES OF ALL TIME

THE 100 GREATEST KIDS RIDDLES OF ALL TIME

100 *MORE* OF THE GREATEST DAD JOKES OF ALL TIME

THE 100 GREATEST KNOCK KNOCK JOKES OF ALL TIME

www.ingramcontent.com/pod-product-compliance
Lightning Source LLC
Chambersburg PA
CBHW061743050726
47598CB00002B/574